MOLD ME PERFECT

"Intimidating Expressions"

By

Macey Brown

Mold Me Perfect

"Intimidating Expressions"

Published by Macey Brown

Dallas, Texas

MOLD ME PERFECT

All right reserved. No part of this book may be reproduced or transmitted in any form or by means, electronic or mechanical photocopying and recording or by any information storage or retrieval system, without permission in writing by the publisher.

The cataloging-in-publication is on file with the Library of Congress.

Library of Congress Control Number

ISBN: 13: 978-1534994478
ISBN: 10: 1534994475

Copyright © 2016 by Macey Brown

Printed in the United States of America
August 2016

Edited by: Marina Jacobs

Book Cover by: Nadia Harris

Model: Jasmine Thomas

JD Westbrook Photography

Genre: Poetry

Email: msmacey.427@gmail.com

Website: http://msmacey427.wix.com/poem

Dedications

This book is dedicated to David Ashby, Dianne Hurt, Kim Cosby, Debra Mitchell, Gladys Jones-Wilson, Angela Moering-Watkins, Joyce Shorter, Nikki Hurt, Kimberly & Mark Brick, Jennifer Henderson, Loretta Burns-Lockhart, Sharon Ward, Akeim Sears, Sheila Pinkard, Motivational Speaker Melvin Alexander and poetry lovers all over the world... "Sistahs With Ink"

Acknowledgements

I would like to acknowledge and give my appreciation to motivational speaker and business entrepreneur David Ashby and associates at **The Best Author's Lounge**. Thank you for allowing me to be a part of an amazing opportunity and an amazing literary group. You all show you care about aspiring writers by providing free training tools, knowledge and motivation to allow them to strive towards their dreams and goals of becoming a writer.

I would like to give recognition and appreciation to my writing coach and mentor, Author Brooklen Borne, my editor, Marina Jacobs and Author Nadia Harris for graphic designs. Thank you for your assistance in allowing me to reach my goal of publishing my second book of poetry. I am deeply grateful.

Author's Notes

"Actions speak louder than words". This is one of my favorite quotes. I often let my actions speak for me on a daily basis and I am very intimidating in many ways. Although I am not perfect, my life purpose is focused on motivating and aspiring others, so I became a writer. It's easier for me to write my feelings, thoughts and emotions down on paper. I spend quality time to write, focus and meditate. As a silent individual, I can become a loner and distance myself for peace and serenity at any given time. My actions and expressions can become very intimidating to some people and perceived in many different ways, often portraying me as being a selfish and vain individual. But I am actually the opposite, with a huge personality and a very kind heart, which is usually mistaken for weakness or vulnerability.

Being intimidating can be misleading and confusing to some, but a type of shield for others like myself. It comes naturally for me to be out spoken and aggressive. Freedom of Speech is a very important right. Knowing who you are is a powerful thing as you influence others, offering positive vibes without intimidating them with fear and negativity.

The poems written in this book are based on several familiar scenarios that some of us face in life. There are some combinations of my characteristics written in my poetry. I include my persona in my writings to be a part of each poem.

Author's Notes cont……..

Welcome to my world of poetic vibes. I get a pleasure from expressing my feeling when writing poetry. Each stroke of my pen flows ink that tells a short story in lyrics with rhythmic notes. I challenge myself as a poetess to take the most extraordinary and unusual words and make them rhyme.

Because of rhythm, I have the talent to rhyme

Because of literature, I can express what's on my mind

MOLD ME PERFECT

Table of Contents

Chapter One: Running Out of Lies

- Issues..Pg 10-13
- Stumbling Blocks..................................Pg 14-15
- Fed Up..Pg 16-17
- Episodes...Pg 18-19
- Before I Walk Away..............................Pg 20-21

Chapter Two: Intimidating Expressions

- Fearless..Pg 22-23
- Bold Intentions.....................................Pg 24
- Outnumbered.......................................Pg 25
- Magnetic Attractions.............................Pg 26-27
- Mold Me Perfect..................................Pg 28-29

Chapter Three: Let Me Introduce Myself

- Hi, My Name Is...................................Pg 30-31
- Intimidating Ways................................Pg 32-33
- Just Being Me.....................................Pg 34-35
- A Beautiful Soul..................................Pg 36-37
- Dear Diary..Pg 38-39

MOLD ME PERFECT

Chapter Four: Envious Thoughts

- That Woman................................Pg 40-41
- She Said What?...........................Pg 42-43
- False Accusations.......................Pg 44-45
- Keeping Secrets..........................Pg 46-47
- Bitch Eyes...................................Pg 48

Chapter Five: Second Chances

- What If..Pg 49-50
- Caught up...................................Pg 51-52
- Letting Go...................................Pg 53-54
- Misled...Pg 55-56
- Sick and Tired............................Pg 57-58

Chapter Six: Thinking Out Loud

- Second Thoughts........................Pg 59
- High Hopes.................................Pg 60
- Wishful Thinking........................Pg 61
- Mirror, Mirror............................Pg 62
- Fairy Tales..................................Pg 63-64

MOLD ME PERFECT

Chapter Seven: **Living Life Gracefully**

- Having Faith……………………………….Pg 65-66
- A Little Prayer…………………………….Pg 67-68
- A Little Hug Will Do……………………...Pg 69
- I Am "Living Life Gracefully"…………Pg 70-71
- Living It Up………………………………..Pg 72-73

Chapter Eight: **Moments of Happiness**

- Smiles……………………………………..Pg 74
- Weekend Blues "All Night Long"……..Pg 75
- My Love Is………………………………..Pg 76
- Memories…………………………………Pg 77-78
- Blessings…………………………………Pg 79-80
- Because…………………………………...Pg 81

Chapter One: **Running Out of Lies**

ISSUES

I have issues
And these issues are running my life
I have issues and problems
That I constantly have to hide

All my sorrows
I have hidden them too
But these issues and problems
I can't break through

These issues are becoming a pest
Like a thorn
In my side
Taking over my thoughts
It's getting difficult to think or decide

These problems and issues
Effects in life
These issues are coming at me
From left and right

I have issues and problems
Sleeping at night
Even in my dreams
I am putting up a fight

MOLD ME PERFECT

These issues are becoming major problems
And getting out of hand
I even have issues
When it comes to keeping a man

These issues have a mind of their own
Ripping apart relationships
And breaking up homes

These issues are problems
I cannot relate
All the drama, insecurities, envy and hate

Issues are problems
We all have to face
Issues can surface
Any second of the day

No time, no warning
No particular place

I have problems with these issues
Getting in my way
I even have issues
Keeping up my good faith

I have issues with interference
Interrupting my space
These problems with issues
Just won't go away

I have issues with lies

MOLD ME PERFECT

And disappearing acts

I have issues with gossip
And talks behind my back

I have problems with issues
Causing disrespect
Accepting forgiveness
I won't settle for that

I have issues with young girls
Having low self esteem
Obsessed with thugs
Low life's and dope fiends

Trapped in domestic violence
Ending up crime scenes

And not to mention
Grown ass women
Doing the same damn thing
Being messy
Keeping up drama
Playing childish games

I have problems with criminals
Taking innocent lives
The loss of little children
Who didn't survive

These issues with poverty
The daily struggles to survive

| MOLD ME PERFECT

The high cost of living
And paying the price

I have issues with
Testing my intelligence

I have problems with anything
That doesn't make sense

Like issues with the poor
Supporting the rich

And problems speaking my mind
Isn't that a bitch!

STUMBLING BLOCKS

I ran into a stumbling block
The other day
I tripped on a hurdle
Trouble got in my way

I was caught off guard
Knocked off my feet
Hitting rock bottom
I was in
Pretty deep

I didn't see it coming
There was nothing in site

Stumbling blocks
Aroused
Interrupting my life

Blindsided and surprised
Halted
In my tracks

Held up
By stumbling blocks
Complications and setbacks

Distractions and obstacles
In my path

MOLD ME PERFECT

Abrupt delays
And coming in last

Stumbling blocks
High barriers and snags
Complicated drawbacks
All from my past

FED UP

Fed up with
Disappointments
And being treated
So cold

The same old situation
This shit is
Getting old

Putting up with
excuses
I won't take this
Anymore

Failures
Being dishonest
Running out of lies and more

Fed up
With problems and drama
From people being rude
With negative conversations
And funky attitudes

The lack of respect
And acting like a fool

Fed up
With life's disappointments

MOLD ME PERFECT

No exceptions
I won't approve

Dirty tricks
Being slick
Lies and being fooled

Fed up
With the lack of respect
Fed up
With all these moods

I refused
To be mistreated
I refused
To be misused

EPISODES

Flashbacks of episodes
Memories from the past
Years of love and happiness
Shattered like broken glass

Written notes in a bottle
Tossed amongst
The sea
Directions to nowhere
As far as the eyes
Can see

Episodes of illusions
Of what life
Use to be

A vision in my mind
Spent in time
Just you and me

Crossroads
Ups and downs
Hard times
We both reflect

And beautiful thoughts
Of love we shared
When no one else was there

MOLD ME PERFECT

Flashbacks of episodes
A lifestyle
Of you and me

Treasures of moments and memories
The path of
What used to be

BEFORE I WALK AWAY

With thoughts
Running in and out
Of my head
Before I walk away
There is more to be said

This is my confession
I must say
Life was a bitch
Pretending in your face

The secret relationships
Lies being told
Many broken hearts
And so much more

Misunderstandings
About this and that
Promises made
That couldn't be kept

No-shows and excuses
I could not bare
And nights spent alone
You were never there

There is much more
I just can't believe
No value of worth

MOLD ME PERFECT

No appreciation for me

But
Before I let you go
Before I walk away

It was all my fault
I let you treat me that way

Chapter Two: **Intimidating Expressions**

FEARLESS

Be bold and courageous
Fearless at all times
Walk in confidence
Have a positive mind

Know your place
Be defined
With who you are

Stand up in a crowd
Be fearless and proud
Stay in your lane
Stick to your vows

Knowledge is the power
The intelligence of knowing how

Have the patience
To be strong
And never step down

Take challenges at all times
And stand your ground

Fearless is having the courage
To be bold
Heroic and brave

MOLD ME PERFECT

Be fearless
In all endeavors

Be fearless
With intimidating ways

BOLD INTENTIONS

A little mischievous
Unpredictable
With shady moods

Aggressive with bold intentions
And nothing to lose

Smiles so innocent
Often misunderstood

Looks so bodacious
With nothing to prove

No competition
A guarantee to lure

With bold intentions
And breaking all the rules

OUTNUMBERED

Always outnumbered
Coming in first
Having pride in values
And testing my strength

Always a winner
Determined to exceed
Reaching for the top
Being the best
That I can be

Lifting spirits
Inspired with skills
Sharing knowledge
With bright ideals

Always focused
Reaching goals
Always outnumbered
And striving for more

MAGNETIC ATTRACTIONS

Passionate with emotions
Too conceited and sometimes vain
Captivating looks
Irresistible with good taste

Alluring with temptations
Bold with provocative ways

Casting seductive spells on me
I am caught up in a daze

Alluring magnetic attractions
Desires and willing
To please

Seductive vibes and intentions
Obsessed in love with me

Captured by magnetic attractions
Possessed with power and greed

A will to satisfy
And actions to meet all needs

The power of attraction
A passion so deep

MOLD ME PERFECT

Being in control
And taking advantage of me

From innocent smiles
To being mistaken as a tease

These alluring and magnetic attractions
Are getting the very best of me

MOLD ME PERFECT

Enter my soul
Uplift me in praise

Mold me prefect
In a special way

Guide my spirit
Take control of my life

Mold me perfect
Mold me right

Capture my heart
Erase all doubt

Mold me perfect
From inside and out

Enhance my beauty
With features like a queen

Mold me perfect
With looks fit for a king

Mold me perfect
With love and grace

Mold me perfect
Each and everyday

MOLD ME PERFECT

Mold me perfect
With a smiling face

Mold me perfectible
In each and every way

Chapter Three: **Let Me Introduce Myself**

Hi, My Name Is

Hi
My name is Beautiful
The one who's sweet and bold
Overjoyed with emotions
And blessed with a heart of gold

Bonjour
My name is Love
The aphrodisiac
"A freak"

I cast spells
On the vulnerable and weak
I am a powerful potion
Of TLC

Please handle me with caution
I break hearts you see

Hello
My name is Joy
I am gleeful
My soul is free

Abundant with love
And my middle name is Peace

MOLD ME PERFECT

I bring smiles to faces
With sadness and grief

Hey
My name is Success
I am simply the best

You can reach the highest levels
By passing my test

Focus on me
And I will handle the rest

Blessings
My name is Faith
I am spiritual and unique

I bring grace and mercy
To lost souls in need of peace

Your prayers will be answered
Have trust in me

INTIMIDATING WAYS

Benevolent smile
With a lovely face
Looks so deceiving
With intimidating ways

Inspired by many
Envied by a few
My intimidating ways
Are making breakthroughs

Taking action
Being observant
Making promises
Enriching the world

Put me to the test
I will do my best
When it comes to confidence
I am above all the rest

My intimidating ways
Are lessons learned
Making changes to lives
One by one

Aggressive with nerves
Outspoken with words
Influence with knowledge
I must be heard

MOLD ME PERFECT

So serious and bold
I have been told
My intimidating ways
Are taking control

JUST BEING ME

There is no other person
I would rather be
Then the one and only
Yes
That's me

There is no other being
In the world like me
Genes are shared
Chromosomes are unique

I am someone special
Lovely as can be

Content with happiness
Of just being me

Like an uncut diamond
A precious pearl from the sea

There is nothing like the joy
Of just being me

Made from love
I was conceived
I broke the mold
An extraordinary breed

MOLD ME PERFECT

Kind and divine
Heavenly sent
Born to give
Equipped with strength

A BEAUTIFUL SOUL

Bright morning sunrises
High waves over the sea
A beautiful soul
Virtuous me

Touched by love
A warm embrace
Bonded for life
I am set in my ways

A beautiful soul
I am highly praised
With nights of holy prayers
Angelic in every way

A life of blessings
I must say
A beautiful soul
Has taken place

Spirits and halos
Angels in flight
Blessing souls
And saving lives

Paving ways
To heavenly stairs

MOLD ME PERFECT

Saying prayers
To get you there

Living life gracefully
Day by day
A beautiful soul
Has taken place

DEAR DIARY

Dear diary
Let me introduce myself
I have something
On my mind
Let me express myself

Dear diary
I am writing
My confessions in you
I am telling it all
And reminiscing on what's true

Hidden skeletons in closets
Revealing intimacy too

Dear diary
I have an ultimatum for you
I am telling it all
With nothing to lose

I am being open
I am confiding in you

Jotting down my thoughts
Written confessions
To view
Words of confidence
Shared between us two

MOLD ME PERFECT

Dear diary
I have a lot on my mind
I need to share my thoughts
I have to write it all out

Dear diary
I am honest with you
Being open
With confessions
And telling the truth

Chapter Four: **Envious Thoughts**

THAT WOMAN

Her look is surreal
Stepping high in heels

Who is that woman?
She has sex appeal

Where is she going?
Dressed up like that

Draped in pearls
Black mink
And matching hat

That short mini skirt
Above her knees
Strutting like a model
She's a flirt
Just a tease

Hands on her hips
Head held high
Walking in confidence
Classy with style

Who is that woman?
Annoying is she

MOLD ME PERFECT

Attitude of a diva
Intimidating as can be

I want to be like her
I wish that woman was me

SHE SAID WHAT?

She thinks she is something
She thinks she is all that
She said what?
Did she really say that?

What did she say?
Did I hear that right?
She is asking for it
She is ready for a fight

He said
She said
Bla, Bla, Bla

Who said what?
She was just saying
That's what I thought

She said what I was thinking all the time
She said what
I wasn't worth a thin dime

Who is she?
What did she say?
I don't know her anyway

She said what
Is there more

MOLD ME PERFECT

Of that he said

She said
What she said
What!

FALSE ACCUSATIONS

False accusations
Playing games
And being slick

Caught up in hard feelings
And having a bone to pick

Being judged on making decisions
Competitions
And making bets

False accusations
Being accused of this and that

Opening old wounds
Being stabbed in the back

Being rude
With bitter thoughts
Walking away
And taking cheap shots

Fake smiles
Bad mouthing
Cursed with negative vibes

Making smart remarks
Pretending and telling lies

Blocked by distraction
And falling apart
False accusations
Being envious and making a charge

KEEPING SECRETS

Making promises
To keeping secrets
Love letters
And hidden affairs

I was running on empty
I was living on edge

Guilty thoughts
Of keeping secrets
Started crossing my mind

Years of misery
And wasting my time
Thoughts of sleepless nights
Weeping and crying

Being conscious
On making confessions
And taking deep breaths
to exhaled

Still running on empty
Still living on edge
Lines being crossed
I am losing my head

Things are out of control
I am clearing the air

Having thoughts
Keeping secrets
And being caught up
In a love affair

BITCH EYES

She has aggressive expressions
With a stone cold face
She has evil bitch eyes
And complicated ways

Her devious smile
Is bold and perturbed
And those evil bitch eyes
Speak louder than words

She's inconsiderate
With inferior ways
Persistent and persuasive
So vain and dismayed

Those evil bitch eyes
And her sinful ways
A wicked combination
Staring face to face

MOLD ME PERFECT

Chapter Five: **Second Chances**

WHAT IF?

What if I was perfect
And had small thighs?

What if I was unfaithful
And living a lie?

What if I was beautiful
But ugly inside?

What if I was rich
And had everything?
Living it up
Like a queen with her king

What if I was dying
Sick in bed?

Would you still love me
Or leave me instead?

What if I was blind
And could not see?

Would you be my eyes
To guide and lead me?

MOLD ME PERFECT

What if my smile was fake
And my feelings
I constantly hide?

What if I was homeless
And living outside?

What if the pain of stress and depression
Led to suicide?

What if you lived a hundred years
Still not satisfied?

And what if I said yes
To share my time?

Spending my life
Right by your side

What if?

CAUGHT UP

Caught up
In between crossroads
Caught up
On which way to go

Caught up in being selfish
Caught up
With no confidence to show

Caught up
In losing a perfect life
Caught up in
Letting things go

Kindness became weakness
Lust took over faith

Lost on a road to nowhere
Caught up
Between love and hate

Standing between crossroads
Having choices to make

Caught up
In a whirlwind
Caught up
In decisions to make

MOLD ME PERFECT

Caught up
In what was good

Caught up
In making mistakes

LETTING GO

A million ways
To say hello
It's hard
Saying good bye

There's no more second chances
No time
For looking back

No time for memories
Of years gone by

It's time to let go
It' time to decide

From all the stress and sorrow
I feel inside
It's time to let go of the hate
I constantly hide

Taking deep breaths
Letting it all
Sink in

And letting go of all things
That make me sin

Letting go

And being able to share my time

Letting go
And accepting forgiveness
Just to have
A piece of mind

Letting go of all pain
I feel inside

Letting go of second chances
Being free
And living my life

MISLED

Hitting rock bottom
Hanging on a string

False impressions
And unpredictable things

Being misguided and led astray
Putting up with manipulations
Day by day

Caught up in betrayal
Blindsided and deceived
False impressions
And being misled

Trapped and controlled
Lost and condemned
Same situations
Stuck and overwhelmed

Falling apart
Catching hell
Down and out
And being misled

Making excuses
Putting up with lies
Being judged

MOLD ME PERFECT

And wasting my time

Being misled
Casted astray
With false impressions
And unpredictable ways

SICK AND TIRED

Putting up with
Accusations
Making excuses
To hide a lie

Sick and tired
Of being the victim
This is it
I will not deny

Putting up with rude intentions
Humiliations and alibies

It's time to get back
My dignity
Self-respect
And having some pride

No room
For cruel situations
Disappointments
And controlling my life

Sick and tired
Of being accused
Sick and tired of being in denial

Sick and tired
Of accusations

Sick and tired
Of all these lies

MOLD ME PERFECT

Chapter Six: **Thinking Out Loud**

SECOND THOUGHTS

Thinking out loud
I was lost for words
Having second thoughts
I was losing my nerves

Caught up in distractions
I was being influenced
Taken for granted
I was about to be ruined

Making decisions
I am ready for the world

Taking action
Speaking up
Staying cautious
And being observed

Having second thoughts
I am thinking things through
No funky situations
And being influenced

HIGH HOPES

Reaching for the stars
As far as the eyes
Can see

A vision of
High hopes
A future built
Just for me

A road to success
A better life
For me

Having high hopes
And to prosper
With ease

Setting my standards
Of comfort to fit
My needs

I have visions of high hopes
and living out my dreams

WISHFUL THINKING

Dazed in illusions
And speaking out loud

Trapped
In my thoughts
I was floating on a cloud

Wishful thinking gave me thrills
And I was mesmerized

Talking
In my sleep
Daydreaming
In between

Tossing and turning
Imagining things

I was having impressions
It all seemed real

Caught up
In my feelings

Wishful thinking
Gave me thrills

MIRROR, MIRROR

Mirror, mirror
Starring back at me

A lovely image of a beauty queen
Photographic
A lovely scenery

Mirror, mirror
Painting a picture of me

A perfection of beauty
A reflection of me

Mirror, mirror
Another side of me

The appearance in my mirror
Looking back at me

FAIRYTALES

Once upon a time
As a child
I would play

I believed in fairytales
Back in the day

Once upon a time
And many years ago

I dreamed of living in fairytales
And castles made of gold

Once upon a time
In a land of kings and queens

I was a princess
A maiden in my dreams

With Knights in shining amour
Rescuing me

Wearing pretty dresses
Laced with ribbons and strings

A magical world of fiction
A life of imagining things

MOLD ME PERFECT

Those were days of childhood
Living in fantasies

All caught up in fairytales
A world of mythological dreams

Chapter Seven: **Living Life Gracefully**

HAVING FAITH

Having faith
In love and happiness

Having faith
When worried and weak

Having faith
In my decisions
And just being me

Having faith
In the Lord
And the strength
To forgive

Having faith
God will bless me
With my desires at will

Having faith
That all the sick
Be at peace and healed

Having faith
That someday cancer
Will be cured

MOLD ME PERFECT

Having faith
To live peacefully
And not in fear

Having faith
In grace and mercy
Throughout my divine years

I have faith in my prayers
With patience to wait
And grow old faithfully
Outliving prejudice and hate

Having faith
When overwhelmed in problems

Having faith
In tears, I cry

Having faith
To accept death
And to never ask why

I have faith
To live life heavenly
Like angles in the sky

A LITTLE PRAYER

I been told that
Life gets better
And time will ease all pain

I been faced with
Trials and tribulations
A little prayer
Got me through these days

It's been said
Wisdom grows with age
And to err is human
In many ways

Some say
There are no tomorrows
And living in the past
Is just a waste

Be wise
In planning a future
And no looking back
On yesterday

I was taught as a child
To always have faith
And to say a little prayer
Each and everyday

MOLD ME PERFECT

I have failed with bad decisions
Making mistakes
Were lessons for me

Saying a little prayer
Got me through these things

A LITTLE HUG WILL DO

When feeling lonely
And spirits are blue

When down and out
A little hug will do

When times get tough
And love turns to hate

A little hug will do
To test your faith

When life is darkening
With heartache and strain

A little hug will do
To cure the pain

I AM "Living Life Gracefully"

I am unpredictable
A bit stubborn
And set in my ways

I am considered a woman
So gracefully
And highly praised

I was born
To be a leader
Determined
And taking challenges to win

I am brave and courageous
Breaking all barriers
In between

I am filled with
Love and hope
I believe in possibilities
And dreams

I am living with inspirations
And setting goals
With visions to succeed

I surround myself
With happiness
My world is built on strength

MOLD ME PERFECT

I am fearless
Living life gracefully
Sharing blessings
Inspired by faith

LIVING IT UP

Living it up
Taking it all in
Giving advice
And loving life for what it is

Setting examples
Sharing wisdom with friends
I am living it up
And taking it all in

Speaking my mind
And keeping it real
Spreading some love
With everything to give

Living it up
And chasing my dreams
Being inspired
With changing things

There is a purpose in life
To give and receive
I am planning my goals
And setting out to achieve

I am living my life
And doing my thing

MOLD ME PERFECT

Rearranging my life
Making amends

I am living it up
And taking it all in

Chapter Eight: **Moments of Happiness**

SMILES

Happiness is a smile
Covered with
Laughter and joy

Smiles are made of love
And so much more

Smiles are very beautiful
From within
Not out

Smiles say hello
Without a doubt

WEEKEND BLUES "All Night Long"

Back in the day
My mother would say
It's the weekend baby
Let's dance the night away

Kicking up my heels
Go put your hot pants on
I feel like dancing
Turn that record player on

I have that spirit
Deep inside my soul
I got the weekend blues baby
All night long

Hold up on that needle child
Don't scratch my record now

Put on some
Oldies and Goodies
Make your Momma proud

I had the weekend blues
Playing my Momma's favorite songs
We danced until
The midnight hour
We use to party
All night long

MY LOVE IS

My love is passionate
A precious gift
Delicate as flowers
Sweet as a kiss

Sharing hugs
Holding hands
Smiles and laughter
Making plans

My love is real
Faithful and true
My love is beautiful
Kind and pure

Keeping promises
Saying I do
Forever and ever
A life
with you

Together again
Hand in hand

Praising together
Halleluiah, Amen

MEMORIES

Memories
Of breaking up
Burning bridges
And getting drunk

Dancing
All night long
Shacking our booty
To the funk

We went on double dates
Listened to music
On eight track tapes

There was back seat kissing
And sneaking home late

Growing up
On the run
Hanging out
And having fun

Kids were teacher's pet
Following all the rules
Some were playing hooky
And even skipping school

Leather jackets were cool

MOLD ME PERFECT

Girls were wearing mini skirts

Boys wore bellbottoms
And white collared shirts

Mood rings were fads
We all did pinky swears
Girls wore ponytails
And pressed out their hair

We jumped Double Dutch
We were raised old schooled
We went roller skating
And hula hooped too

Growing up
On the run
Hanging out
And having fun

Breaking up
Raising hell
Burning bridges
And getting drunk

BLESSINGS

Blessings to the weary
For they shall weep
Blessings to all
Who pray for me

Blessings to the sun
And a moon so bright
Blessings to raindrops
Falling from the sky

Blessings for the dawn
Of another day
Blessings to the old
And their elderly ways

Blessings for the love
Of family and friends
Blessings to the sinners
Being born again

Blessings to the lonely
Homeless and sick
Blessings to all in poverty
With needs

Blessings to the young
With a heart of gold

MOLD ME PERFECT

Blessings to all
With beautiful souls

BECAUSE

My will to achieve
Is my biggest fight

My love for poetry
Led me to write

Because of literature
We learn to read

Because of knowledge
We have the power to succeed

I am setting goals
And meeting my needs

And because of purpose
I am living out my dream

Author Macey Brown

Made in the USA
Coppell, TX
22 October 2025

61651512R00046